Small gestures of
endurance

Published by Penteract Press, 2024

PenteractPress.com
PenteractPress@gmail.com
X.com/PenteractPress

Cover design, content, and layout by Rachel Smith
Collection copyright © Rachel Smith

Typeset in Baskerville

FIRST EDITION

ISBN 978-1-913421-48-9.

Rachel Smith is a Sheffield-based artist and visual poet whose work spans drawing, writing, and photography. She co-edits intergraphia books with Emma Bolland. Her work is collected in a range of anthologies and poetry libraries both nationally and internationally. Recent works include: *Stopping Or*, a handmade artist book as part of the AMBruno *Intervals* project, 2024; *Read(writ)ing*, a section translated into Finnish by Tuli & Savu, 2023; *Breath:e St(utter)ance*, an artist book published by Timglaset, Sweden, 2023; *Promise the Infinite: drawing out Babel*, an artist book published by Penteract Press, UK, 2022.

rachelartsmith.com
@rachel_artsmith

Small gestures of endurance

RACHEL SMITH

Contents

for Her

furniture was confounded

she remembered
a sprig
on the tablecloth

fragment I |: equivalents

[...]
[...]

fold | unfold | fold | crease

the event is long since ended but it clatters
around this house
clinging
to equivalents

upholstered corners are grazed by abrasive walls
standing rigidly silent

pleasure comes from jumbling the order of space
disorientating time

there had been a little sprig or leaf pattern on the tablecloth
which she had looked at

a moment of revelation

I search for the tablecloth

finding instead my grandmother's appliquéd pillowcase
tracing tiny stitches. needled. fabric. repetitively. pierced

fold | unfold | fold | unfold | fold

hope might be found in those little daily miracles

I watch her. move. she remembers. the significance. of
that. moment is. lost. until much. later. a penny drops

the object is remembered. imagined
                    remembered
                    imagined

                              is remembered but the thing I possess
          is a lie
             no
          synonym

I wish. it held up. to their scrutiny. it is too large. too heavy. it
does not align. with a delicacy. they. understand. I am undone.
accepting. her telling. of history. stories. handed down. filtered.
the scent of fag ash told as roses. I cling. to presented versions.
as if they will be enough

they tut

unfold | fold

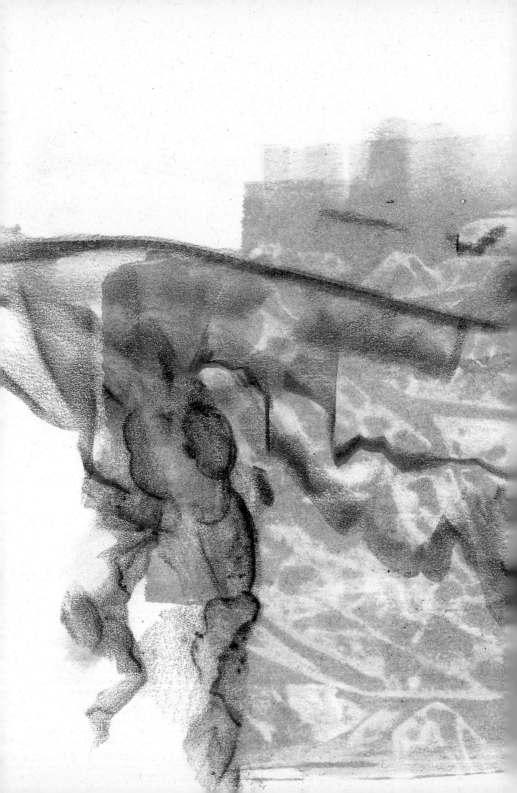

Lily thought

Lily stepped back

Lily asked herself

Lily thought

Lily thought

Lily smiled

Lily wondered

Lily cried

Lily squeezed

Lily thought

Lily thought

Lily looked up

Lily got up

perhaps she was thinking of herself as the person in the book

fragment II | : bodies

[…]
[…]

I is but a convenient term for somebody who has
no real being

                                        I am devoured by the text

She might yet be more real
They will be constructed

You find yourself   fragmented
[…]
I am beside myself
[…]
She gets ahead of herself
[…]
They are not themselves
[…]
I don't recognise myself

                    all bodies are each other

they turned away from the view

She is turned around

lost

reading relentlessly through the full stops

re-orientate. reside

take. up. space

situate

where. what. who. is Your orientation?

why do You return here still
trying to put things back   in place

a place for everything and everything in its   place
                        I am out of   place

She feels. people. spending time. trying to tidy. Her. away. so that
Her sharp. incongruous edges. do. not. show. it seems odd that. She
tolerates. Their. incessant. need. to neaten. to make. everything.
match

mask

I lean into Her shadow
                    the inevitability of Her skin Her papery knuckles are
mine as bodies tally up genetic histories

fold | unfold | fold | unfold | fold |
                        I am folded away

she did not see it like that

struggling against terrific odds to maintain her courage

but this is what I see
this

hopelessly discontented

a remnant of her vision

things appear more clearly with eyes closed

but I cannot make Her see

I look up
caught in Her gaze watching Me remember Her ability to disappear
while standing in front of You is uncanny

She turns away

emotional black holes inhale

Lily thought
Lily thought
Lily contrasted
Lily felt
Lily felt
Lily wanted
Lily thought

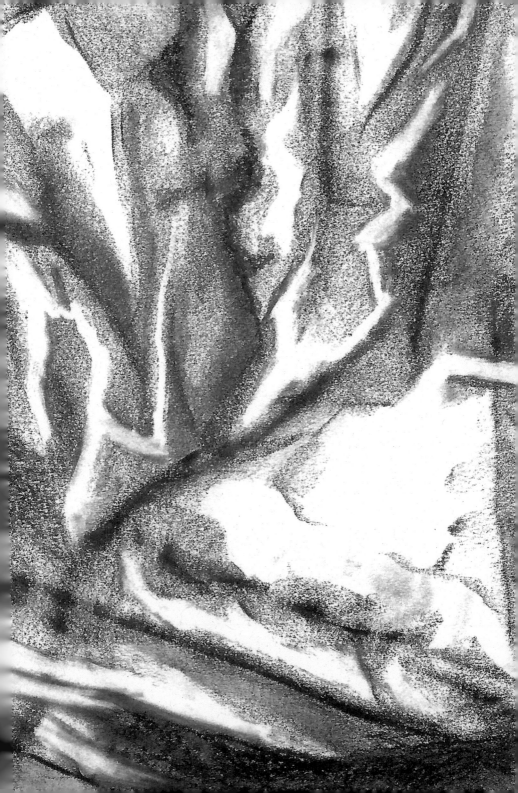

mopping and scouring

fragment III | : polished surfaces

[…]
[…]

a veneer of politeness is maintained by frequently
repeated
applications
of polish

they always longed for
          hated

                    superficial acceptability

skin pressed into cotton. layered. flecked felt. protecting. polished
wood. cotton toes. flexed in-amongst knotted rag scraps. layered.
over newspaper. insulating. wooden boards

unfold | fold

she saw it clear for a second

there, in

                                 the centre

incidents gather
fibres cling to faded stains

surfaces
hold contact
objects resurrect their past lives

                              scrubbed surfaces erode
                  arm-deep in buckets of diluted bleach
                            with scuffed nylon knees

words are being woven
                  biography of the tablecloth

                  psychogeography

                              her tilted head
                  listens to the fabric of the building

            forcefully flicking dust from the yellow cloth

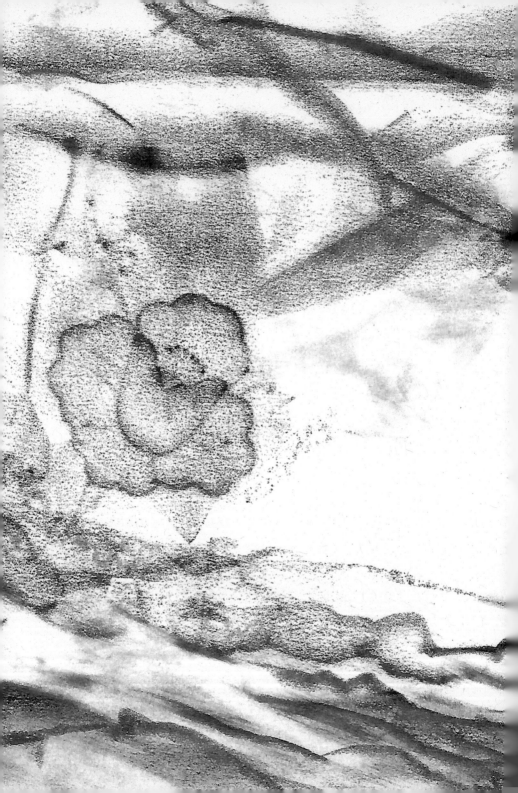

Lily thought
Lily thought
Lily said yes and no
Lily saw
Lily felt
Lily forgot
Lily reminded herself
Lily believed
Lily rose
Lily reflected

she took it up
she put it down   again on a flower

in the pattern
in the tablecloth

her eye caught the salt cellar

fragment IV |: shards of glass

[…]
[…]

prismatic slivers
    cling to shadow edges

                    greys shift through pink blue
yellow below the fading window

she hands her the vase. I hug. glass. curves. bracing. under the
weight. she sweeps firmly at cotton creases. they remain

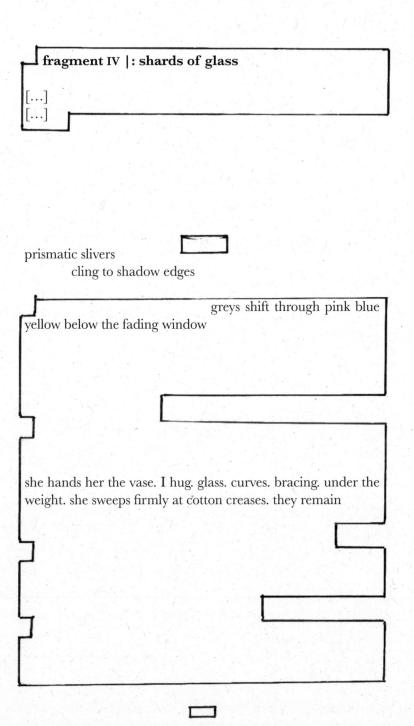

at any rate, she said to herself, catching sight of the salt cellar on the
pattern, she need not marry
thank heaven

weeds that had grown close to the glass in the night tapped
methodically at the window pane

she leant out of the window

edges of the rhythmic diamonds are glimpsed into sharp contrast. her crumpled squint brings little relief. perilous glassy edges catch me. off. guard. unexpected. deluges choke

glass slumps under a cloudy filter
her shadow
shrinks
a stain mellows

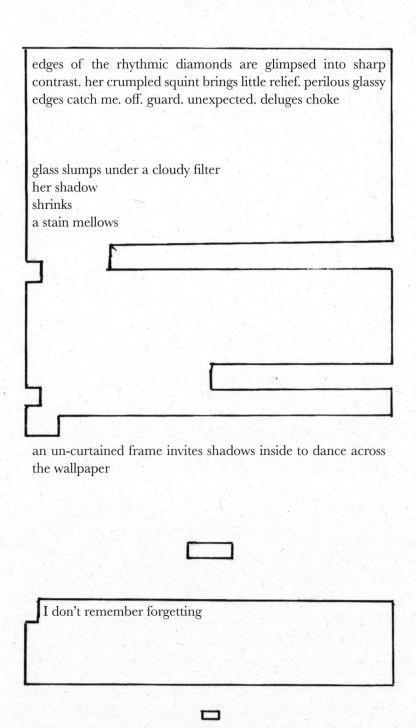

an un-curtained frame invites shadows inside to dance across the wallpaper

I don't remember forgetting

said Lily
said Lily
said Lily
said Lily
said Lily

stories of my birth
always emphasised a glassy view

beneath streaks of purple moorland

she never read *Wuthering Heights* but clasped close
torn fragments
of Kate Bush

rain taps at the smeared pane

breath against misted glass
water dribbles between the panes
she longs to break the vacancy in the foreground

sat. looking out. looking in. looking through. looking beyond

Lily thought
Lily supposed
Lily knew
Lily looked
Lily thought
Lily felt
Lily felt
Lily wanted
Lily could see
Lily thought
Lily laid

Lily was tired
Lily heard
Lily asked herself
Lily wished
Lily said nothing
Lily wished
Lily thought
Lily flew into a rage
Lily decided

and again she felt alone

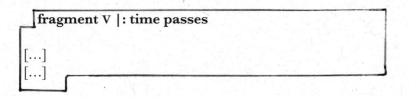

fragment V | : time passes

[...]
[...]

familiarity wears away. resolve. the stale smell of cigarettes weaves itself in amongst the cotton threads slowly marking a yellowish stain across the delicate pattern. a heavy wooden candlestick. oddly. placed   to the left. hides a frayed moth. eaten. edge. a tiny   hole

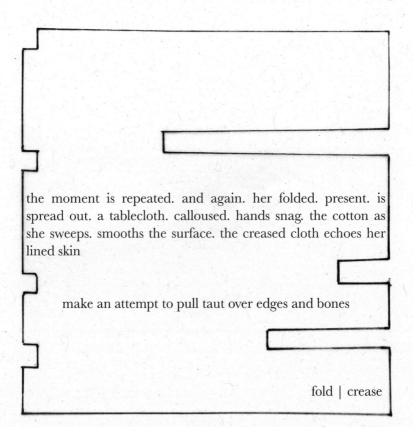

the moment is repeated. and again. her folded. present. is spread out. a tablecloth. calloused. hands snag. the cotton as she sweeps. smooths the surface. the creased cloth echoes her lined skin

make an attempt to pull taut over edges and bones

fold | crease

the books and things were mouldy

a dog-eared photograph slipped between the pages of a book
a
marker
a
reminder

she wondered about its significance

stop. one sixtieth of a second. a chipped bowl of sickly ripened cherries rests on the crumpled cloth. shadows gather in the sagging folds. a relentless prickling surface which makes it hard to think. the eye clicks it was like reading a good book again, for she knew the end of that story the smell of dust drifts upwards

squeeze the page between thumb and forefinger

mouth the words
trace a line of the words with a finger

cradle the spine in a palm

find a place to stop
she opens the book wide and pauses puting it face down

skin is paper
her words press against my surface
leave a scar

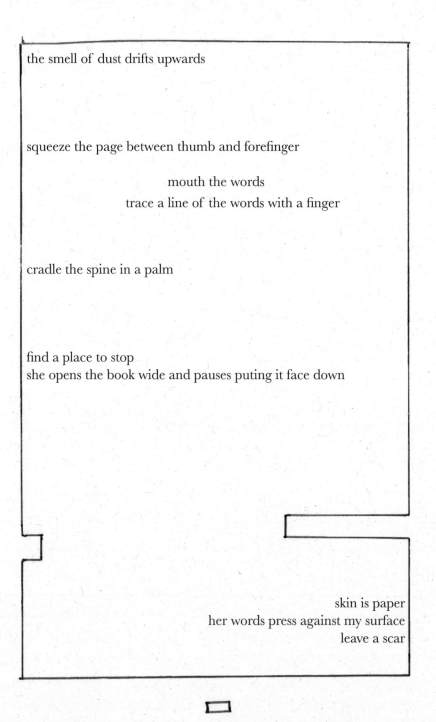

she left the house shut up, locked, alone

wooden signs board up an empty space. hand-painted names
brutally collaged. exposed. progress. unwittingly reveals. dirty
laundry. a public hanging.

you are dangled

without warning
blush
but
they do not care. I do not. know. only. you are thrown.
off. balance

the fog of inevitability obscures much needed detail

lies do not blink
they crawl
from open mouths

she feels nothing but destruction

fold | unfold | crumple

and as she dipped into the blue paint
she dipped too into the past

his grip squeezes the past to the surface
muscle memory stiffens your response

all water suddenly salty
she gasps for air

drawing
 drowning
drawing
 drowning

how can I tell when the end is nearing?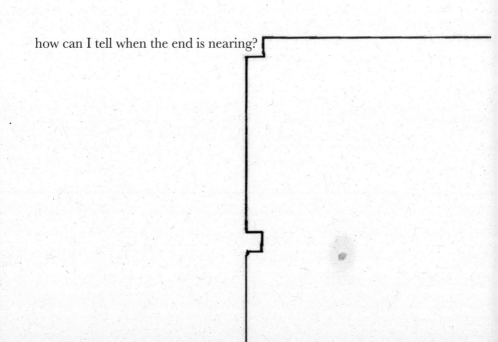

the wind blew from the worst possible direction

materialised in greyscale colour profile discarded

the small of her back pressed into the cold papered plaster hoping
to vanish into the sealed cavity between the walls

to exist unseen
unheard

I spoke only in my head

aguey hands fret

Lily thought

Lily is so fond of flowers

she laid the flowers on the table while she dusted

fragment VI | : floral tributes

[...]
[...]

I long for. blousy blooms. peonies. hydrangeas. not cowed by
her bitter suspicion of white lilies. harbingers. she blames the
yellowed stains on fallen pollen. nicotine. pollen. nicotine.
pollen. shapes and structures of longiflorum trumpets offer a
grandeur. she sold to others. a sickly. smell. hands plunged into
swampy water. plastic vases to be scrubbed. clean

browning crisp edged petals deftly plucked
refresh the faces of ageing roses
thorns
stripped from stems

she spits. barbs. hereditary. rage.
seething. on both sides. skips a generation. lodging needles in
fleshy surfaces. wounding. if disturbed. take. shallow. breaths
[...]

the wallpaper was flapping

        you couldn't tell anymore that those were roses

        she let her flowers fall

        violets came and daffodils

now deeply. inhale. exhale. revealed by smoke a long sigh that drifts. upwards. clinging. to the wallpaper. beneath. the flowery layers. long forgotten faces. are inscribed. they watch on. silently. as layers of faded fabric daisys. are. stripped. away. to make room

planted in haste
            by
          sparrows
undernourished sunflowers
raise their heads
between
stones craning their necks towards the sun

a bruised camellia. plucked. carried. discarded. trodden into asphalt

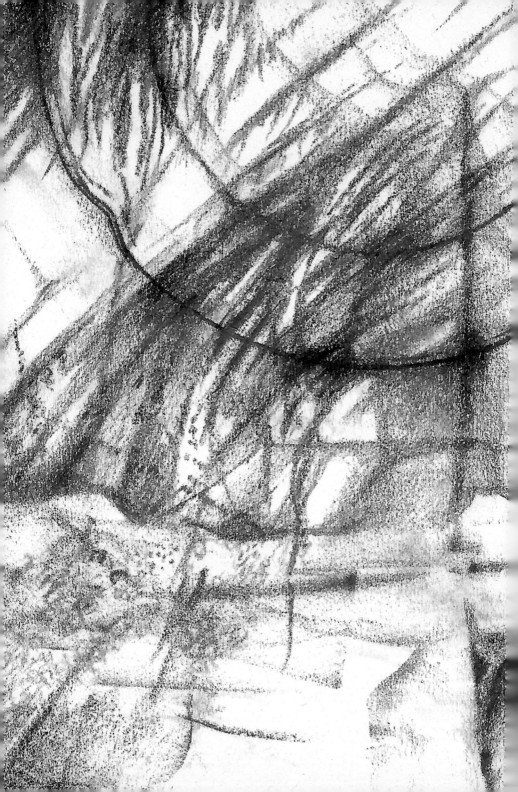

Lily thought
Lily felt
Lily forgot

a shadow was on the page

fragment VII | : camouflage

[...]
[...]

I was unspeakable and ran into the language of others

a sheep in Woolf's clothing
she attempts to climb inside and walk around

tightly folded between desk and chair
the persistently blinking cursor disapproves
lines disintegrate

her words. clatter. in my mouth awkwardly. clumsily. bumping
poking uncomfortably   stuttering
                              tuttering
                              tutt

                              tut

                              tut
                              tut
                              tut

Lily thought

Lily watched

Lily thought

Lily thought

Lily thought

Lily thought

they must keep the windows open and the doors shut

a sense of doors slamming

the wall staring white

fragment VIII | : opening. closing

[...]
[...]

closed. open. movement seems impossible

defeat in stillness

she thought how unpleasant it is. to be. locked. out. while you thought. perhaps. it might be worse. to be. locked. in

cornered

doors that keep her in
doors that keep her out

doors held open
yet. slammed. shut. before she can. cross. the threshold

she opens the book and began reading here and there at random

the night was now shut off

she had locked the door; she had gone

pages longing for sunlight. sealed in silence

(t)here

a book remains closed
words and annotations pressed closely together

it is my fault

she remembered

I catch her breath as she need not breathe

what did she wish to indicate by that triangular purple shape
just there

marginalia crowd together. they point

she sits
they point
a dried biro falters. the nib stumbles. into a papery surface. I have
let my guard down. doubt. spreads. a juicy stain soaking through
fabric recklessly colouring beyond the outlines of the patterned
tablecloth

she adds another line
a pencil point crumbles under pressure

she brushes off shadows of doubt
smudges remain

writing. from room to room. order. structure. they did not match
her waking reality

the unsettling interiority of rooms whose doors have been removed

                                                          dislocation

awkward spaces
  blank spaces
  small spaces

                                        she was stuck in a room

reading closed books

incompleteness begs to be finished

she remains
unfinished

a desire to be left without an ending

unfold | unfold | unfold

a refusal to be tolerated

slide a scrap of paper between us. between the pages.

to remind me

to forget

fold | crease

I turn the page

[...]

[...]

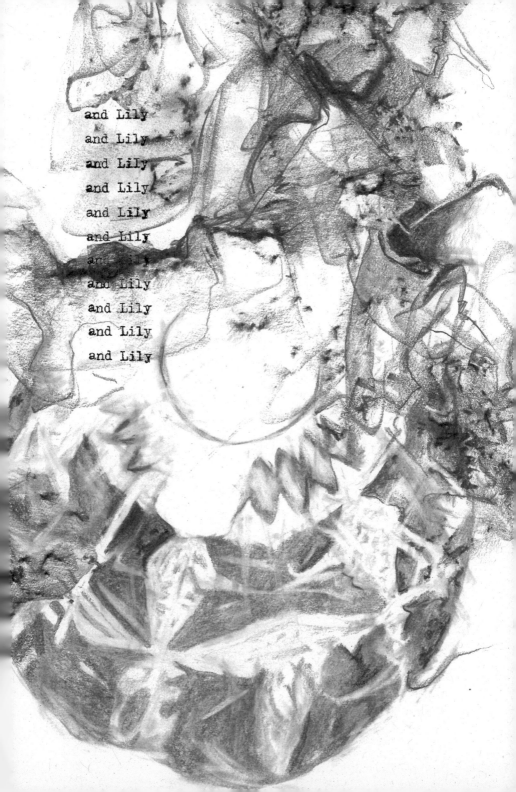

and Lily
and Lily
and Lily
and Lily
and Lily
and Lily
and Lily
and Lily
and Lily
and Lily
and Lily

Afterword

Put simply, the publication and bound nature of this book enable me to take a breath from my near five-year preoccupation with Virginia Woolf's *To the Lighthouse*.

This volume of accumulated fragments might be considered as an archive of associations; a layering and folding of domestic histories; a valuing of polite embroidered surfaces to distract from the smell of fag ash and swampy vase water; a process of fighting the creeping doubts handed down and across generations; an insolent but smitten neurodiverse reading; a noticing of minute movements.

an almost
imperceptible
act of resistance

Why Woolf? is a question that returns. In trying to resolve an answer I read Charlotte Perkins-Gilman, Erin Manning, Maria Fusco, Georges Perec, Sina Queryras, Hélène Cixous. I drift through 'A Room of Ones Own' and dwell on spaces, rooms, walls, pages, tablecloths, and the significance of that salt cellar.

There is a moment in Woolf's novel where artist Lily Briscoe moves a salt cellar across the tablecloth. The action is slight, an unnoticed event.

She picks it up.
She puts it down.
Placing it onto a particular detail in the patterned tablecloth, resting it on a leaf sprig.

a reminder
a reminder of how to resolve a work in progress
a reminder to avoid the expectations of normative structures

I reflect on hyperfocus

Tiny details block out the noise. An act of noticing. Small gestures.
Echoes. The practice of moving things around.

make room
make space
        space to breathe, to
make

Acknowledgements

Many heartfelt thanks go out to:

Monica Oechsler (ed) with Sharon Kivland at MA Bibliothèque for including my work in their anthology *Salon for a Speculative Future*, 2020. A celebration of Women's History Month, this collection acts 'as a platform for cross-generational and cross-disciplinary exchange'. My contribution *Catching Sight of the Salt Cellar* was the initial spark for the work contained herein.

Julia Calver for inviting me to present a very early version of this work at *The Writing for Practice Forum* as part of the peer-led research collaboration between Goldsmiths College and Sheffield Hallam University. And to Karenjit Sandhu, invited guest respondent at the session, whose generous and critical insights were incredibly valuable in the early stages of this project.

Emma Bolland, who invited me to perform a fragment of this work at her event *Speaking Architectures: an evening of creative and critical readings* as part of her *Thinking architectures* exhibition at the Post Office Gallery in Sheffield.

Joanna Jowett and Charlotte Morgan at Copy [copypages.org], who published an earlier and smaller fragment of this work in their litho-printed publication *COPY // unfold II*, 2023.

Anthony and Clara at Penteract Press for their support over the years, both to myself and to the wider community of amazing people they have brought together.

The varied circle of brilliant and generous artists and writers who I am lucky to have in my life. They have listened, supported, and offered invaluable feedback while I wrote, drew, and performed seemingly endless fragments of these pages.

My neurodiverse friends who see.

All of these encounters have enabled me to persevere with the process of constructing and deconstructing this unfinished work.